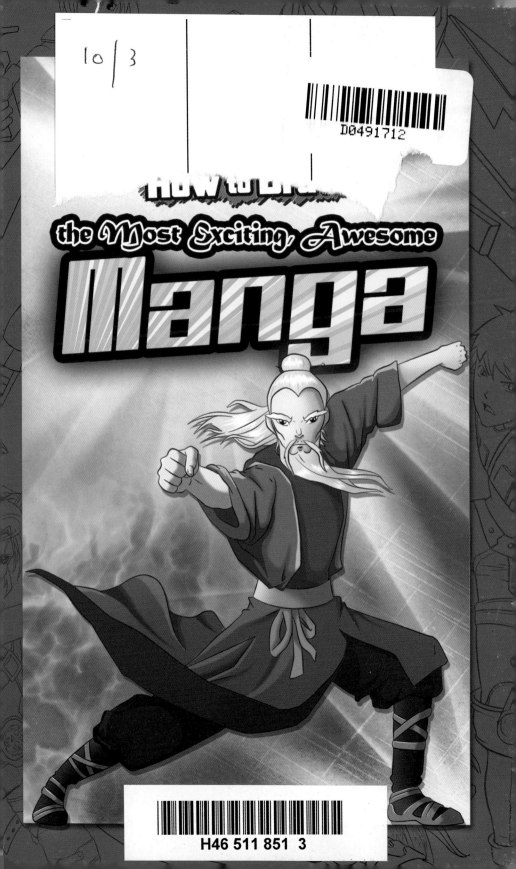

HOW to DRAW

the Most Exciting, Awesome

Manga

www.raintreepublishers.co.uk
Visit our website to find out
more information about
Raintree books.

To order:
☎ Phone 0845 6044371
📄 Fax +44 (0) 1865 312263
📠 Email myorders@raintreepublishers.co.uk

Customers from outside the UK please telephone +44 1865 312262

Raintree is an imprint of Capstone Global Library Limited, a company incorporated in England and Wales having its registered office at 7 Pilgrim Street, London EC4V 6LB
Registered company number: 6695882

ISBN 978 1 406 24292 8 (paperback)
16 15 14 13 12
10 9 8 7 6 5 4 3 2 1

British Library Cataloguing in Publication Data
Singh, Asavari.
How to draw the most exciting, awesome manga.
741.5'1-dc23
A full catalogue record for this book is available from the British Library.

Author: Asavari Singh
Editor: Laura Knowles
Art Director: Joita Das
Designer: Deepika Verma, Isha Khanna, Navneet Kaur
Colouring Artists: Aadil Ahmed Siddiqui, Abhijeet Sharma, Danish Zaidi,
Priyanka Singh, Madhavi Poddar, Vinay Kumar Sharma
Line Artists: Deepak Kumar, Ishan Varma, Martin James, Nishant Mudgal,
Prithwiraj Samat, Surendra Kumar Tripathi
Originated by Capstone Global Library
Printed and bound in China by Leo Paper Products Ltd

Disclaimer
All the internet addresses (URLs) given in this book were valid at the time of going to press. However, due to the dynamic nature of the internet, some addresses may have changed, or sites may have changed or ceased to exist since publication. While the publisher regrets any inconvenience this may cause readers, no responsibility for any such changes can be accepted by the publisher.

CONTENTS

Chapter 1

What is MANGA?

Unique style, powerful poses, and amazing action are what manga comics are all about. They are packed with cool characters, too, ranging from awesome warriors to fearsome robots and a whole lot more.

Manga is a style of drawing that became popular in Japan in the 1940s. The word manga means "whimsical pictures" in Japanese, but this art form is about more than just drawing. It is also about storytelling, distinctive themes, and powerful characters. Today, manga is a worldwide phenomenon that you can be a part of, too!

All about style

Manga characters have a very distinctive look. They are less realistic than other comic book characters. They usually have large eyes, small mouths, pointed chins, and funky, colourful hair.

Chapter 2

Pieces and Parts

Let's start with the typical manga head. First you'll learn to draw the front and side views and see how features are placed. Then have fun with hairstyles and accessories!

FRONT VIEW

 Draw a circle and cut it in half with a vertical line. Then draw three lines to divide the head. Extend the vertical line to mark the chin's tip. Draw the jaw and neck.

Use the horizontal lines as guidelines for placing the hairline, eyebrows, eyes, and mouth.

Add details to the eyes. The nose and mouth come next – remember, these are never very detailed. Complete the outline of the hair.

Erase all unnecessary lines. Add more detail to the eyes and hair. You can even add highlights to the hair in typical manga style!

PROFILE

1 Draw a divided circle for the profile. This time, though, the chin will slant sideways from the circle. Add features and hair.

2 Finish the eye and hair. Erase guidelines.

HAIR

Hairstyles can tell you a lot about a manga character. Traditional down-to-earth characters usually have long straight hair. Young energetic characters often sport short, spiky hairstyles. The wilder the hair, the wilder the character's personality!

Eyes and expressions

The eyes are the most important part of a manga character's face. They really have to pop, so pay attention to detail. The nose and mouth are a breeze in comparison!

1 Draw guidelines across the face. Then place two U-shapes for the eyes on either side of the face.

2 Draw a long oval within each eye. Define the upper and lower edges of the eyes.

3 Draw the eyebrows and define the upper lid as shown. Draw an oval within each oval. Add sparkle to the eyes by defining light glares in each eye.

4 Darken the eyes. Leave some parts white to show shine. Add sweeping eyelashes. Erase guidelines.

Show different emotions by adjusting the shape of the eyes and eyebrows.

ANGRY

CALM

WORRIED

SHOCKED

SAD

IRRITATED

Tip

Males generally have narrower eyes than females, while children have the roundest peepers.

Hands and feet

Hands and feet can be a little tricky to draw. So practice making the basic shapes well. Once you do this, you'll be able to draw hands in many gestures and positions.

 1 Make a wireframe for the hand, with a square palm and circles for knuckles.

2 Draw around the lines to flesh out the wireframe.

3 Add details such as fingernails and knuckles.

Try these expressive gestures. Make sure you start with a wireframe.

Try to draw the foot from different angles. You can also dress it up with different kinds of footwear.

1 Make a *trapezium* shape for the foot. It should be broadest at the toes. Draw a line for the ankle.

2 Draw tube shapes around the lines for the toes. Draw arcs near the tips of the toes.

3 Define the final shape of the leg and add details such as the toenails and heel.

trapezium: four-sided shape that has only one pair of parallel lines

Chapter 3

Body Basics

A simple stick figure (also known as a wireframe) is the skeleton of any manga body. It helps define the size, proportions, and shape of a character. You can then layer on all the flesh and fashion you want.

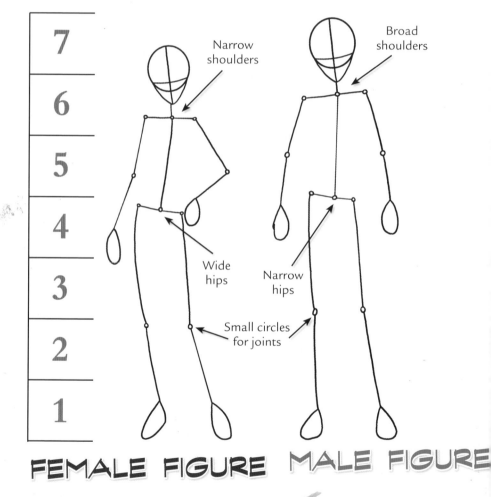

Narrow shoulders

Broad shoulders

Wide hips

Narrow hips

Small circles for joints

FEMALE FIGURE   MALE FIGURE

It's important to get your proportions right. Manga men are about seven heads tall, while women are around 6.5 heads tall.

proportion: size of one part in relation to another

Flesh out your stick figures with solid shapes such as spheres, cylinders, and curved rectangles. This will give them a three-dimensional look.

Tips

- Don't use perfectly straight lines for human shapes. Lines will be more curved for female shapes.
- Use the joints to guide your proportions. The arms and legs will taper off from these points on the body.
- Read up on human anatomy and look at pictures of how different muscles drape over the bones. This will help you draw more accurately.

sphere: three-dimensional or solid circle, like a football

Dynamic posing

Experiment with the wireframe to create exciting action poses. This is known as **dynamic posing**.

Dynamic poses are almost always drawn at an angle. This gives the character a three-dimensional look.

Kneeling characters are tricky to draw. Before starting, see how different body parts overlap.

Watch out! This fist is coming at your face! Use a technique called foreshortening to show perspective – the arm looks compressed and the fist is larger.

Martial arts poses are popular in manga. The front punch and back kick is a classic.

Chapter 4

Details, Details

Make your drawings come to life with costumes, accessories, and smart shading. Get creative!

Wardrobe basics

Clothes make the man – and manga! Outfits and accessories make an instant statement about different types of characters, so get ready to play fashion designer.

1 **Everyday outfits:** Young, happy-go-lucky characters like to lounge about in jeans and loose T-shirts. Draw folds and creases where there is movement. Folds are loose on the baggy jumper but tighter on the jeans.

2 **Armour:** Warriors are fond of strong protective gear and **elaborate** belts. They are rarely seen without a weapon of some sort.

elaborate: with lots of details and decorations

3 **Capes:** Capes are popular with female characters, although certain males will wear them too. Add designs at the neck and the hem.

4 **Boots:** Boots are necessary for kicking hard. Make them big and bold. Add straps and studs.

5 **Metal:** Make solid armour equipped with high-tech features for robots and futuristic characters.

shading

You can work magic with black, white, and grey. Shading is key to adding depth to your drawings and giving them a three-dimensional look. It also helps add texture.

Light and shadows

Imagine a light source – such as the bulb shown here – before you begin shading. The part of an object that the light hits stays white, while the rest is shadowed. Do you notice how the same light source illuminates different shapes differently?

Tips

- Shadows vary according to the shape of the object and the placement of the light source.
- Start shading about halfway down the object. Note that this rule changes for cubes and spheres.
- You can shade with colour, too. Just use lighter or darker hues of the same basic colour.

illuminate: to light up, or make bright with light

Try to catch the play of shadows and light on your character's body and clothes.

1 When the light shines from one side, the parts of the body facing the source appear bright. The parts facing away will be in shadow.

2 When the light falls from above, the exposed surfaces are illuminated. The inside of the umbrella is dark so a shadow is cast over the head and shoulders. Pay attention to the **contours** of the body and clothes as you shade.

contour: curve or outline of a shape or object

Chapter 5

HEROES AND HEROINES

The heroes and heroines of manga comics have several features in common. They are tall, slender, good-looking, and have large eyes that indicate their honest nature.

Traditional hero

Dragons tremble and ladies go weak at the knees when this dashing warrior arrives.

1 Start with a stick figure in an action position. Make small circles for the joints in the body.

2 Flesh out the body with curved lines and draw bigger circles for the kneecaps and elbow. Outline the sword.

3 Armour, a large belt, boots, and a dagger are a must for a traditional hero. Add details to the face.

4 Add details to the clothes, weapons, and accessories. Mark the folds and creases that appear on his clothes as he gets ready to strike. Complete the face. Once your final sketch is ready, rub out any remaining guidelines.

Tip

Use hard number-three (H3) pencils to make the first two stages of the drawing, since these are easier to erase. Use number-one or number-two pencils to sketch the final outline.

5 Colour your hero. Clothes and accessories in green, grey, and brown give the warrior a military look. Draw a simple background. Some moonlight will add lots of drama. Make sure the sword glints.

6 Take colouring a step further by carefully shading your drawing. Add white tints to the hair to make it shine. Use different shades of the same colour on the costume. Brighter tones show where light is falling.

Modern warrior

With guns and eyes blazing, the modern warrior is a **formidable** foe. He can be quite sneaky sometimes, but he always does the right thing in the end.

1 Draw a stick figure. The warrior is crouching slightly, ready to shoot. Let the spine curve downward.

Tip

Give your warrior a pointed chin and narrow eyes. The leaner and meaner he is, the more exaggerated these features should be.

2 Give bulk to the warrior. Draw a circle for the hips, letting it overlap the waist and thighs. Flesh out the limbs.

3 Get your warrior ready for action by drawing details of his armour and boots. Draw his eyes and outline his hair.

formidable: powerful, inspires fear

4 Add more details to the guns, costume, and boots. Shape his hair and features and give him a snarl.

5 Add colour. This warrior has sleek, state-of-the-art guns – in shiny black, of course! He straps his lightweight protective gear over an ordinary pair of jeans and a shirt. That way, he can blend in with the crowd to make a quick getaway after fighting the bad guys.

Warrior princess

Warrior heroines are a force to reckon with! These combat queens have a softer side, too. You can see it in their flowing locks and stylish accessories!

1 Begin with a stick figure. The heroine is poised to attack, so draw the head, arms, and legs in an action pose. Draw a curved line for a deadly twin-blade sword.

2 Flesh out the body. The hips will be wider than those of male figures.

3 Add details to the clothes and eyes. Then shape her hair so that it flows behind her. This will add movement.

4 Add details to her clothes and hands: a victory sign should work well. Complete the deadly sword. Don't forget to give your heroine a triumphant smirk!

5 Colour your drawing. Offset her steely blade and shoes with a feminine gold belt buckle and dressy bracelets. Use fiery red, orange, and maroon for the clothing.

6 Finally, shade your drawing. Add tints of white to her hair to give it a lively shine. Specks of white in the pupils will give her eyes a determined glint. Make sure to shade her skin, too.

Modern heroine

With her eyes always on target, this pistol-toting heroine means business. She's a bit of a tomboy and rarely lets her hair down.

 Your heroine has just burst into a room full of villains, so give the stick figure an aggressive pose. The hand facing you should be bigger than the other.

2 Flesh out the body with a circle for the hips, a long and slender waist, and powerful legs. Draw the outlines for her guns.

3 Dress her up in a flowing cloak, and let her hair fly in different directions. This will give movement to the character.

4 Add details to her face, hair, and body. Define her muscles. Mark out creases on the clothes.

Fact

An entire genre of manga is devoted to "girls with guns".

5 Tough girls can wear pink, too! And when you have guns like that, a ribbon balances things out nicely. Make sure you draw folds in her cloak and highlights in her hair for a more realistic look.

Chapter 6

SPECIAL CHARACTERS

The main protagonists are supported by a vast and varied cast of supporting characters.

Sensei

The sensei (grandmaster) is no spring chicken, but he can run rings around the fiercest young fighters.

1 Draw a stick figure in a fighting position, with legs apart and arms raised to the sides.

2 Flesh out the stick figure. Remember, the sensei is a rather wiry fellow. Draw circles to define the joints.

3 Give your sensei a samurai-style hairdo. Make his wispy beard flow in the opposite direction. Dress him up in martial arts clothes.

protagonist: lead character of a story

4 Add details to the hair and face. Don't forget the bushy eyebrows! Once your final outline is ready, rub out the guidelines.

Tip

Older faces have more defined cheekbones and the eyes are deeper set.

5 This old warrior's eyebrows are as grey as his hair and beard. Keep the colours simple, but be sure to bring out the folds in the clothes. The creases on the sleeves and tunic help add movement.

Mecha

Mecha are robots with a human touch – they are piloted by people. They can squash everything in sight, shoot weapons, and even perform martial arts stunts.

1 Draw a stick figure. Your mecha should be poised to attack, so extend one leg and arm way out. Keep the other leg bent.

2 Geometric shapes are the building blocks of the mecha. You can even use a ruler to get those lean, mean lines right.

3 No mecha is complete without some serious armour. Add thrusters at the back. Make sure the arms are pointed backward. This posture brings force to your drawing.

Fact

A giant statue of a mecha from the anime series *Gundam* watches over the city of Shizuoka in Japan. The 18-metre (59-foot) statue is equipped with a beam sabre that lights up at night.

4 Add details to the mecha. You can go as high-tech as you want with the look.

5 Colour the mecha. Add touches of grey to give it a metallic appearance, but don't be afraid to use colours for different parts of his gear.

6 Use colours to highlight details, such as the mini control box on his wrist and the disguised weapon case on his leg.

7 Metallic surfaces reflect light strongly, so use lots of white tints on the mecha's body. Make two thin, white outlines around the body to add a force field around the mecha. You need to show he's all charged up!

Chibis

A chibi is a cute little creature with a large head and tiny body. The body, feet, and hands are very basic, but the eyes as well as the hair can be wild and expressive. Sometimes, normal characters transform into chibis for a short while. This happens when they feel extreme emotions.

Tip

Chibi characters have a body-to-head **ratio** of about 1:1. A normal child's ratio is approximately 4:1.

CHIBI GIRL   NORMAL GIRL

ratio: number of times one quantity contains another similar quantity

A chibi's eyes take up most of its noseless face.
They tell you all there is to know about the character.

DELIGHTED

WORRIED

SAD

SNEAKY

Fact

A chibi causes lots of drama and excitement but its antics don't affect the main story.

TIRED

Magical girl

She's cute but ordinary until one day – boom! She discovers she has special powers. These could range from being able to fly to casting magic spells.

 1 Draw a stick figure. This girl is flying, so her legs should be raised and bent.

 2 Flesh out the body. The circle to show the hip will be small since the girl still has a childish body shape.

3 Add a magic cloak, wings on the shoes, and a cute magic wand. The eyes should be very round to show her innocence.

4 Add final details to the outfit and hair. She should look surprised but happy!

5 Finally, add colour. Think bright and girly. Red hair with golden tints sets her apart from the crowd. Add a magical glow around the wand.

Fact

The inspiration for the magical girl genre in manga came from the 1960s hit American TV series *Bewitched*. It became popular in Japan as well.

Chapter 7

THE BIG PICTURE

It's time to make a manga comic! Once you decide on your characters and story, make a storyboard. Then simply add details and words.

Arrange panels according to the scenes and situations you want to show. Make a rough sketch of your characters.

Flesh out your characters, adding details as you go along. Keep the background simple so that the focus stays on the characters. Fine lines around a character help show action and excitement.

Add drama with colour and shapes. The splashes of red on a black background represent the fight between the hero and the dragon. This adds drama and a more sophisticated look.

Fact

In Japan, manga is read from right to left! This format is often followed in Western countries as well.

Use your imagination – and speech
bubbles – to complete your story.

Zenada is the last princess of the Kagaza kingdom.
All her six sisters have just been killed by Aagakha, the
dragon. She runs into the forest and stumbles into the
arms of outlaw-warrior Shomo.

What do we
have here?
Looks like a
baby lizard.

The forest turns orange, then red. Aagakha breathes out giant flames, but Shomo knows a trick or two. He leaps up and sticks his sword up Aagakha's nostrils. The dragon goes up in flames. Aagakha has been slain.

That wasn't so hard. The dragon is now dra-gone!

Find out more

Books

The Art of Drawing Manga, Ben Krefta (Arcturus Books, 2009)

Macbeth (Manga Shakespeare), Robert Deas (SelfMadeHero, 2008)

Manga (Trailblazers), David Orme (Ransom Publishing, 2006)

The Saga of Darren Shan series (manga edition), Darren Shan, illustrated by Takahiro Arai (HarperCollins, 2009)

Warriors series (manga edition), Erin Hunter (HarperCollins and TokyoPop, 2008)

Websites

**www.howtodrawmanga.com/howtodraw/
tutorials.html**
Visit this website from the "Manga University" to find lots of helpful tutorials on how to draw manga.